Stillness in Storm

Finding Meaning in a Distracted Age

Acknowledgment

This book, *Stillness in the Storm*, is not merely a collection of thoughts, but a reflection of the inner journey I have undertaken a journey shaped by grace, guided by love, and nurtured by silent strength.

First and foremost, I bow in humble gratitude to the **Almighty**, the infinite presence that has been my anchor through seasons of clarity and confusion, silence and noise. In moments when I felt lost, it was divine stillness that called me back to myself.

To my **beloved parents**, thank you for the unwavering support, quiet wisdom, and unconditional love. Your values have shaped my conscience, your strength has fortified my spirit, and your belief in me has been a steady compass even when I faltered.

To my **loved ones** those who have stood beside me, challenged me, held space for me, and inspired me your presence has been a gentle yet powerful reminder that even in the storms of life, love remains the most grounding force of all.

This book exists because of your light.
Thank you for being my shelter, my stillness, and my storm.

With heartfelt gratitude,

Arghyaraj Basu

About the Author

Arghyaraj Basu is an advocate by profession and a seeker by spirit. Passionate about the deeper truths of life, he combines his legal acumen with a profound interest in philosophy, spirituality, and human psychology. Through his writing, he seeks to bridge the gap between the inner and outer worlds between contemplation and action, between stillness and the storm.

His previous work, ***Awaken Through Karma***, offered a fresh perspective on duty, consciousness, and self-transformation, resonating deeply with readers seeking purpose in the modern age. In Stillness in the Storm, he continues his exploration this time inviting readers into a deeply personal and universal quest for meaning amidst the chaos of a distracted world.

When he's not practicing law or writing, Arghyaraj enjoys reflecting in quiet spaces, engaging in thought-provoking conversations, and walking paths where silence speaks louder than words.

CONTENTS

Introduction

Stillness in the Storm: Finding Meaning in a Distracted Age

"*In the midst of movement and chaos, keep stillness inside of you.*" — *Deepak Chopra*

There is a peculiar paradox to modern life: we are more connected than ever, yet more isolated; informed, yet confused; stimulated, yet hollow. We scroll endlessly through curated feeds, multitask through shallow moments, and fill our silence with noise yet beneath all this, many feel a quiet ache, a question whispered in the spaces between pings and pixels:

What is all this for?

In a world where time moves faster than thought, where stillness is mistaken for laziness, and depth for irrelevance, the pursuit of meaning has become a rebellion. The storm we face is not just external it rages in the mind, in the soul, in the fractured attention we carry through each day. But amidst that storm, there lies a hidden path: a return to **stillness**, not as escapism, but as truth.

This book is a journey back to that center.

The Age of the Storm

Imagine waking up, reaching for your phone before your feet touch the floor, already immersed in messages, updates, and deadlines. You're not alone billions start their day this way. But this isn't just a habit; it's a symptom. We are drowning in inputs, yet starving for insight.

The storm is real. It is made of:

- **Notifications** that fragment your focus
- **News cycles** that inflate your fears
- **Busyness** disguised as purpose
- **Endless choice** that breeds confusion

Yet the deeper problem is not the external storm. It is the silence we've forgotten to listen to.

The Crisis Beneath the Surface

Sociologists now refer to our era as the "meaning crisis." More people are feeling existentially lost, even when everything appears fine on the outside. We suffer from what the philosopher Søren Kierkegaard once described as the "sickness unto death" the despair of not being in touch with one's own self.

We chase success, visibility, speed but often at the cost of soul, depth, and presence.

This is not new. Ancient sages knew this inner turmoil. But unlike today, they cultivated disciplines of reflection, purpose, and dharma. They sought to align life with **truth**, not trends.

The Call to Stillness

Stillness is not merely the absence of noise; it is the presence of something greater. It is the space where the inner self speaks, where intuition awakens, where meaning reveals itself. It is the quiet in which the soul begins to remember what it has forgotten.

In this book, we will explore:

- How to reclaim your attention and align it with purpose
- Why stillness is not passivity but power
- How ancient wisdom from Vedanta to Stoicism can guide modern living
- Real stories of transformation from chaos to clarity

- Practices to anchor meaning in daily life

An Invitation

This book is not a manual; it is a mirror. It won't give you a rigid formula for purpose, but it will offer something more valuable a way to begin listening again. Not just to the world, but to your own depths.

If you feel something missing amid your achievements…

If your mind is constantly full but your heart feels empty…

If you long for more than productivity for presence, peace, and purpose…

Then this is your invitation.

Let us begin not by speeding up, but by slowing down. Not by doing more, but by being more aware. Let us step into the storm not to be swept away, but to discover the stillness that has been waiting within you all along.

Chapter 1: *The Noise Within and Without*

"All of humanity's problems stem from man's inability to sit quietly in a room alone."
— Blaise Pascal

There was a time not too long ago when silence was a natural part of life. It greeted you in the early morning hours, lingered in the spaces between conversations, and wrapped itself around twilight like a soft blanket. Now, it has become a luxury few can afford or even recognize.

We live in an era where **stillness feels unnatural** and **distraction is the norm**. But the cost of this is far greater than missed moments or fleeting focus. The noise both outer and inner is slowly detaching us from the very core of who we are.

The Outer Storm: A World on Overdrive

Step outside your door or simply open your phone and you'll enter a whirlwind of motion:

- The hum of traffic and the rush of notifications
- Headlines screaming for attention
- The constant pull of messages, likes, and alerts

We are surrounded by what the French sociologist Jean Baudrillard called **"the hyperreal"** a world where simulation replaces substance. Our screens show us polished images of lives not fully lived, while our own lives pass in a blur of swipes and refreshes.

Real-life vignette:
Mira, a 32-year-old marketing executive, once described her daily life as "a slideshow of tasks with no soundtrack." From Zoom calls to social media updates, she performed with efficiency but felt "hollow, like I was watching myself act." One evening, after a panic attack in the middle of a client call, she finally shut everything off and sat quietly on her balcony. The silence was deafening at first. But it was also the first honest moment she'd had in months.

The world outside is loud, yes but it is merely a mirror.

The Inner Noise: A Mind in Turmoil

Even in quiet rooms, our minds race. We rehearse past conversations, catastrophize about tomorrow, compare ourselves to others, judge, justify, regret. We try to sleep, but the mind performs an encore.

This inner noise is not random. It's the *unprocessed residue* of unexamined living.

- The pressure to "be someone"
- The fear of falling behind
- The unresolved wounds we carry silently

"The mind," wrote the Buddha, "is a wonderful servant but a terrible master."
In our distraction-driven culture, the mind is constantly hijacked by algorithms, by conditioning, by fear. We have not only lost silence we have lost command of our own attention.

Why This Matters: The Cost of Constant Noise

What is the price we pay for this endless storm?

- **Shallow relationships** – We scroll past people instead of sitting with them
- **Creative burnout** – Constant input kills original thought
- **Spiritual starvation** – No silence, no soul connection
- **Existential confusion** – Always moving, never arriving

The worst part? We begin to **mistake noise for meaning**. Busyness becomes a badge of worth. Constant communication masquerades as connection. Yet, something deeper in us knows the truth.

A Hidden Wisdom: What the Ancients Understood

Long before smartphones, sages across cultures warned about the mind's tendency to scatter. In the *Bhagavad Gita*, Krishna speaks of the *"chanchala manas"*, the restless mind, which needs steady practice (*abhyasa*) and detachment (*vairagya*) to become still.

The Stoic philosopher Marcus Aurelius advised himself daily to “be like the rock that the waves keep crashing over. It stands unmoved and the raging of the sea falls still around it.”

These weren’t poetic sentiments they were survival tools for the soul.

The Beginning of Return: Awareness

We cannot silence the storm all at once. But we can begin to see it.

Awareness is the first act of rebellion. When we pause even briefly and simply observe, we regain power over the chaos. We create space. And in that space, **something ancient and eternal begins to breathe again**.

Live example:
Arun, a software developer, started spending just five minutes each morning without his phone no agenda, just observation. At first, he described the experience as “itchy.” But within a week, he began to notice birdsong, the feel of sunlight, the rhythm of his breath. “It was like I had been deaf and now I could hear again,” he said. His stress levels dropped. His focus returned. His sense of presence deepened.

Reflection: Are You Listening?

- When was the last time you sat in complete silence, without needing to do anything?
- Can you tell the difference between internal stillness and boredom?
- What thoughts fill your mind when all the outer noise stops?

Write them down. Not to judge but to observe. Awareness is the first sacred step.

Closing Thought

The noise is not your enemy. It is your teacher.

It tells you what you've been avoiding. It reflects what the world has convinced you to believe. But it is not who you are. Beneath the noise beneath the storm—there is a place untouched by chaos.

A place where meaning waits like a lamp in the dark.

In the next chapter, we'll explore **what we've forgotten** in our quest for stimulation and how the search for meaning begins not with answers, but with remembering.

Chapter 2: *The Great Forgetting*

"In the age of information, the greatest challenge is not access but remembrance."
— Anonymous

We live in remarkable times. A world where information is a tap away, where we can see the sunrise over Tokyo and the protests in Paris without leaving our rooms. Yet, for all this connection, something vital is slipping through our fingers.

We are forgetting.

Not facts or passwords but something deeper.
Something quieter.
Something sacred.

We are forgetting **what it means to be fully alive**.

A Subtle Loss

This forgetting doesn't happen all at once. It sneaks in slowly, like fog over a lake. One day, you realize you haven't watched a sunset in months. You can't recall the last time you had a real conversation without checking your phone. You can't remember the last time you felt *present* truly *here*.

And when life finally quiets when the noise settles you notice a soft ache inside, like the memory of a song you once knew by heart, now fading.

The World That Keeps Us Spinning

We wake up and reach for our phones before we even stretch. We scroll past hundreds of images, voices, and opinions before we've had a sip of water. There's always something playing, something buzzing, something asking for our attention.

But in all this rush, all this stimulation, we rarely ask the simplest questions:

- *Why am I doing all this?*
- *What truly matters to me?*
- *Where did I lose myself in the chase?*

Real-life moment:
Priya, a 29-year-old software engineer, once told me, "I was achieving everything I thought I wanted promotions, trips, recognition but I couldn't shake the feeling that I was on autopilot. I was succeeding at a life I never stopped to choose."

What We've Forgotten

We haven't just forgotten how to be still.
We've forgotten how to *feel*, how to *breathe*, how to *be*.

Here's what many of us are quietly losing:

- **Wonder** – The ability to marvel at ordinary beauty
- **Depth** – The patience to sit with hard questions, not rush past them
- **Attention** – The gift of being fully here, not half-there
- **Joy** – Not the kind bought or posted, but the kind that sneaks up on you when you're at peace

And most importantly, we've forgotten that **we are more than what we produce**.

A Glimpse from the Past

Live example:
One afternoon, Rahul, a busy architect in his forties, was visiting his childhood village. As he walked past the old banyan tree, he saw two kids laughing as they floated paper boats in a muddy stream. "It hit me," he said. "This was happiness. No Wi-Fi. No plans. Just this moment." That day, he sat with them no agenda, just presence. He said it was the first time in years he felt truly human again.

Sometimes, what we need is not something new but something old, something familiar, something we left behind without realizing it.

What the Sages Always Knew

Across centuries, the world's great teachers whispered the same message:

You are not incomplete. You have simply forgotten who you are.

In the Bhagavad Gita, Krishna gently reminds the lost warrior Arjuna that he is more than his confusion he is eternal, unshaken, a soul beneath the storm.

In Buddhism, the journey to enlightenment isn't about becoming something else. It's about **waking up** remembering what's always been there.

Even modern science shows us that practices like mindfulness and silence don't "add" something to us they **reveal what's** already within.

How Do We Begin to Remember?

We don't need to change our whole lives overnight.
We begin small. Gently. Kindly.

Try this:

- Sit quietly for five minutes in the morning no phone, no music.
- Take one walk a week with no destination, just to *notice.*
- Light a candle and just watch the flame.
- Ask yourself: *What did I love doing before the world told me what to love?*

Live example:
Amara, a 35-year-old teacher, started a "no-distraction hour" at home every Sunday. No screens. Just books, tea, conversation, or sitting quietly with her thoughts. "It was awkward at first," she laughed. "But now it's sacred. My kids and I talk more. I feel more grounded for the whole week."

Remembering doesn't have to be dramatic.
It can be soft, slow, and full of grace.

A Gentle Reflection

Take a deep breath and ask yourself:

- What moments recently made me feel truly alive?
- What have I left behind that my soul is still calling me toward?
- When was the last time I felt still... and okay with it?

These questions are doorways. Don't rush through them.
Let them open something within you.

Closing Thought

This chapter isn’t about judgment it’s about homecoming.

You haven’t failed. You haven’t lost your way.
You’re simply being called to remember.

To remember the joy of simplicity.
The richness of presence.
The sacred rhythm of being human.

Because beneath all the noise, the rush, and the roles you are still here.

Still whole.
Still waiting.
Still remembering.

Chapter 3: *Purpose Is Not Productivity*

"The trouble with the rat race is that even if you win, you're still a rat."
— Lily Tomlin

We live in a culture that confuses **doing** with **being**, **speed** with **value**, and **output** with **meaning**.

From a young age, we are trained to believe that our worth lies in what we produce, achieve, or accumulate. The world applauds efficiency, celebrates busyness, and rewards performance.

And yet, even when we check all the boxes, climb all the ladders, and hustle through every open door many of us still feel… empty.

Why?

Because purpose is not the same as productivity. Because a meaningful life cannot be measured in metrics.

The Productivity Illusion

Productivity tells us to:

- **Do more** in less time.
- **Maximize** every moment.
- **Optimize** every routine.

But purpose whispers:

- *Slow down.*
- *Feel more deeply.*
- *Live with intention.*

Live example:
Riya, a digital marketing executive, was praised for her hustle 12-hour days, constant results, glowing reviews. But one night, as she stared at the ceiling after another "successful" campaign, she felt a crushing hollowness. "I was moving fast, but toward what? I realized I didn't know why I was working so hard."

We are not machines. We are meaning-makers. And meaning cannot be mass-produced.

The Difference Between Doing and Being

- Productivity is **external** it's about results.
- Purpose is **internal** it's about resonance.

A painter may spend hours lost in color, not thinking of sales.
A teacher may change a life with a simple word of encouragement.
A parent may rock a child to sleep and never call it an achievement yet it's one of the most profound acts of love.

"Not everything that counts can be counted. And not everything that can be counted, counts."
— William Bruce Cameron (often misattributed to Einstein)

The Hustle Generation

We live in an age where the hustle is glorified. We're told to **monetize our hobbies**, **stack our schedules**, and **grind without complaint**.

But hustle without heart is just noise.

Live example:
Kabir, once a rising tech entrepreneur, sold his startup at 33 and achieved what many dream of. But after the deal, he experienced something unexpected: despair. "I thought success would fill the void. It didn't. What I needed wasn't another project. I needed to find myself."

The world may celebrate your success, but only your soul knows whether it was worth it.

A New Definition of Purpose

Let's reimagine purpose not as a finish line, but as a **felt sense of alignment**.

Purpose is…

- What brings you alive.
- What gives you peace.
- What leaves you more *you* at the end of the day, not less.

It's the quiet sense that your life is not just full but **fulfilled**.

It doesn't have to be grand or glamorous.
It just has to be true.

Ancient Clarity

In the Bhagavad Gita, Krishna tells Arjuna:

"Better to fail in one's own dharma than to succeed in another's."

Dharma doesn't mean job. It means **soul alignment**—your true path.

You can be a janitor and live with deep purpose.
You can be a CEO and feel completely adrift.

What matters is not your title but your **truth**.

Reclaiming Purpose in Everyday Life

You don't have to quit everything and move to the mountains.
Begin where you are.

Ask:

- What kind of work makes me feel alive—even when no one is watching?
- What moments in my week feel rich, even if they're small?
- What would I still do, even if it never made money or gained attention?

These questions don't always yield easy answers. But they do open doors.

Live example:
Devika, a former investment banker, left her high-paying job to become a potter. "People thought I'd lost my mind," she laughed. "But for the first time, I feel like I'm in rhythm with my own life. The clay listens to my hands. And I listen to my heart."

Purpose isn't a strategy. It's a **feeling**. A deep yes in your bones.

A Gentle Reflection

Try journaling on this:

- *If I had all the money and approval I needed, how would I spend my days?*
- *What parts of my current life feel forced or performative?*
- *What do I need to stop doing not because I'm failing at it, but because it doesn't feel like me anymore?*

These questions aren't about abandoning responsibility. They're about **remembering why you began**.

Closing Thought

You are not a machine. You are not a number.
You are not here to endlessly optimize yourself.

You are here to *feel*, to *create*, to *love*, to *connect*, and to *mean something* to yourself and to the world.

Let your days be rich with intention.
Let your life be full of soul, not just speed.

Because in the end, it's not about how much you did.

It's about how deeply you lived.

Chapter 4: *The Noise Outside, the Silence Within*

"When the world roars loud, it is the quite soul that truly hears."
— **From 'The Noise Outside', The Silence Within**

Modern life is loud. The world shouts. Our minds echo. Our hearts forget their own rhythm.

We are surrounded by noise of traffic, timelines, opinions, and endless notifications. And beneath it all, a question grows quieter by the day:

When did we last hear ourselves think?

The Tyranny of Noise

Noise today isn't just sound it's saturation.
It comes in forms that seem innocent at first:

- The endless scroll of curated lives.
- The compulsion to respond immediately.

- The invisible pressure to "stay updated" at all costs.
- The news cycles, the pings, the algorithms that never sleep.

We no longer sit with silence we flinch from it. We fear the blank space in a conversation. We fill every pause. We multitask through moments that were once sacred.

Real-life reflection:
Aarav, a 28-year-old consultant, once told me, "I can't sit still for five minutes without music or YouTube. It's like my brain starts to panic in the quiet."

But this fear of silence is not natural. It's trained. And what's trained… can be untrained.

Silence Isn't Emptiness

Silence is not a void. It is the **container of truth**.

It is in silence that:

- The mind clears its fog.
- The heart speaks.
- Creativity whispers.

- Inner wisdom stirs.

Every tradition has honored silence as sacred:

- In **Zen**, silence is the doorway to awakening.
- In **Christian monasticism**, silence is the voice of God.
- In **Hindu dhyana**, it is the space where the Self is revealed.
- In **Sufi mysticism**, it is the music between the notes of the divine.

Silence isn't nothing. It is everything we've forgotten.

A Story from the Forest

There's a story from the Indian Upanishads about a young boy, Nachiketa, who goes to the house of Death to find truth. There, in the stillness beyond fear, he hears what no one else dares to seek.

"The Self is not known through study or intellect, but only when the mind is quiet and the heart is pure." – *Katha Upanishad*

In the deepest stillness, he meets the eternal within himself.

The Constant Stream

The average person today consumes **over 74 GB** of information daily the equivalent of 16 movies. Yet, we still feel starved for meaning.

Why?

Because consumption is not nourishment. Because knowing everything about the world doesn't help if you don't know yourself.

Modern example:
Priya, a schoolteacher, shared, "I was so proud of being 'always online' until I realized I wasn't present for my own life. My students, my family… even my own feelings felt distant."

The noise had become her identity. She chose, slowly, to disconnect for 30 minutes a day. "It's not easy. But now, I actually hear myself."

Listening to the Silence

There is a silence beneath the noise of the world. It lives in:

- The early hours before the city wakes.

- The rustle of trees after rain.
- The breath between thoughts.
- The space between two heartbeats.

It's always there. Waiting.

And the more we listen, the more we realize
this silence doesn't make us feel empty.
It makes us feel **whole**.

The Practice of Inner Stillness

You don't need a cave in the Himalayas to find peace.
You need only a few minutes of **intentional quiet**.

Try this:

1. **Morning Pause:** Before you check your phone, sit in silence for 3 minutes. Let the day meet *you*, not the other way around.
2. **Walking in Silence:** No headphones. Just your footsteps and the world.
3. **Digital Sabbath:** One evening a week, turn off all devices. Light a candle. Read, reflect, rest.

4. **Mindful Listening:** Have a conversation where you speak less and listen with your whole presence.

You will begin to notice the layers of noise peeling away and something gentle emerging underneath: **clarity**.

Real-Life Example: The CEO Who Sat Still

Rajesh, a successful tech CEO, began a silent retreat tradition every quarter no screens, no speech, no meetings. Just solitude.

He says, "Those 48 hours are the most productive days of my year. Not because I get things done but because I remember what matters. I come back with sharper vision and a softer heart."

This is the paradox:
Silence doesn't slow you down. It recalibrates your direction.

A Gentle Reflection

Ask yourself:

- What noises am I letting in without question?

- What am I afraid I'll hear in the silence?
- What would happen if I stopped... for just a moment?

Often, the answers we seek don't come from more data but from deeper listening.

Closing Thought

In a world addicted to volume, stillness is a rebellion.
But it's also a return. A coming home.

The noise outside will never fully stop.
But the silence within is always available
soft, spacious, sacred.

Go there.

Sit awhile.

There, in that hush between the world and the soul, you may find not just peace…

…but yourself.

Chapter 5: *Loneliness in the Crowd*

"The eternal quest of the human being is to shatter his loneliness."
— **Norman Cousins**

We have never been more connected and yet, we've never felt so alone.

The digital age promised us a global village. Instead, it gave us timelines without touch, likes without love, and conversations without presence. We scroll past thousands of faces every day, and still lie awake at night craving to be seen, heard, and held.

In a crowded world, **loneliness has become the silent epidemic.**

Together, But Not Truly With

You can be in a room full of people and still feel invisible.
You can have hundreds of online friends and still feel unknown.

Real-life moment:
Mihir, a college student, described sitting at a table with his friends, all staring at their phones. “We were together,” he said, “but we weren’t *with* each other. It was like being ghosts in the same room.”

This is the loneliness of our times **not the absence of people, but the absence of presence.**

Digital Closeness, Emotional Distance

We are drowning in updates, and starving for intimacy.

We mistake notifications for connection.
We confuse followers with friendships.
We assume that visibility means we’re not alone.

But true connection is not bandwidth. It’s **bond**.

It’s not the blue checkmark next to your name. It’s the quiet voice that says: *I see you. I know you. You matter.*

Loneliness does not come from being alone. It comes from being unable to communicate the things that seem important to you.
— Carl Jung

The Psychology of Loneliness

Psychologists tell us that loneliness doesn't just affect the heart it affects the whole system:

- It elevates stress.
- Weakens immunity.
- Increases anxiety and depression.
- Shrinks our sense of identity and self-worth.

And paradoxically, the lonelier we feel, the more we withdraw, intensifying the very isolation we long to escape.

Ancient Cultures, Ancient Connection

Before skyscrapers and smartphones, community wasn't a luxury it was life.

- In tribal societies, **evening fires** were places of shared stories.
- In villages, **the well** was a sacred social hub.

- In ashrams and monasteries, **satsang** the company of truth was cherished.

These were not transactional relationships. They were spiritual woven with mutual presence, support, and meaning.

We were not meant to go through life alone.
But neither were we meant to lose ourselves in the crowd.

The Paradox of Aloneness and Solitude

There is a difference between **loneliness** and **solitude**.

- Loneliness is the pain of being disconnected.
- Solitude is the power of being inwardly whole.

Solitude heals.
Loneliness hollows.

Example:
Anika, a 45-year-old artist, used to dread being alone. After her divorce, silence terrified her. But over time, she began walking in nature, painting without agenda, and journaling her truth. "I found

that being alone didn't mean I was unloved," she said. "It meant I had space to love myself."

Building Meaningful Connection

To heal from loneliness, we must shift from **connection through convenience** to **connection through courage**.

That means:

- Having fewer, deeper conversations.
- Being vulnerable without performance.
- Asking questions like "How are you *really*?"
- Listening without needing to fix.
- Reaching out even when it's awkward.

We must risk being *seen*, not just being *liked*.

Real-life reflection:
Farhan, a young entrepreneur, made a rule for himself: No shallow texting. Once a week, he'd call an old friend and have an unfiltered,

unscheduled chat. "At first it felt weird," he admitted. "Now it's my soul's oxygen."

Creating Inner Companionship

Sometimes, we search for others to fill the emptiness we haven't yet made peace with ourselves.

This chapter invites you to:

- Become your own steady friend.
- Treat your thoughts with kindness.
- Learn to sit with your feelings without judgment.
- Find joy in your own breath, your own company.

This is not loneliness it is **wholeness**.

"If you are lonely when you're alone, you're in bad company."
— Jean-Paul Sartre

Gentle Reflections

Ask yourself:

- Am I more afraid of silence… or of being truly seen?
- Who in my life truly hears me when I speak?
- How can I show up more fully for myself and for others?

You don't need a thousand people to feel connected.
You need a handful of souls who know your truth and with whom you can be fully human.

Closing Thought

In this age of relentless chatter and curated lives, choose what's real.

Sit with someone and look into their eyes not their screen.
Share a moment that isn't captured.
Speak a truth that isn't edited.

Because the answer to loneliness is not more noise.

It's more **nakedness of heart**. More **reverent listening**. More **soulful presence**.

And sometimes, the most powerful thing you can say to someone is:

"I am here. And I see you."

Chapter 6: *The Myth of More: Why We Keep Chasing What Doesn't Fulfill*

"You can never get enough of what you don't really need to make you happy."
— **Eric Hoffer**

We live in an age of pursuit.
More things. More goals. More speed. More upgrades.

We're sold the dream that happiness lives just beyond the next milestone
the next salary bracket, the next house, the next follower count.

But here's the uncomfortable truth:
More is not the answer.
Because often, more is what distracts us from what truly matters.

The Hunger That Doesn't End

From the time we are young, we are told:
"If you want to be happy, be successful.
If you want to be successful, achieve more.
And if you want to be admired keep climbing."

So we begin chasing:

- Degrees and job titles
- Wealth and social approval
- Relationships that look perfect on the outside
- Possessions that fill our shelves but not our souls

And when we get what we wanted, we feel… a momentary high.
But soon enough, the question returns:
"What's next?"

Real-life reflection:
Rishi, a marketing executive, once said, "When I bought my first luxury car, I thought I'd arrived. But within a month, I was already eyeing a better model. It never ends."

The Illusion of Arrival

We think there's a final destination where all doubts will disappear.
Where we'll feel *complete*, finally.

But life is not a straight line toward contentment.
It is a spiral. A deepening. A return to the center.

The Greek philosophers called it the **hedonic treadmill**
the tendency to return to a baseline of dissatisfaction, no matter how much we achieve.

What if the ladder we've been climbing… is leaning against the wrong wall?

Ancient Wisdom on Contentment

The sages of old knew something we've forgotten:

- Buddha called craving the root of suffering.
- The Gita teaches **nishkama karma** action without attachment to results.
- Stoic philosophers urged us to reduce our desires, not multiply our possessions.

They all pointed to the same truth:
Peace comes not from having more, but from needing less.

"He who is not contented with what he has would not be contented with what he would like to have."
— Socrates

Real-Life Simplicity: The Story of Meera

Meera, a 37-year-old freelance designer, lived a life many envied. Stylish apartment, buzzing social life, a six-figure income. Yet, she felt hollow. "I was consuming experiences like checklists," she said. "Nothing made me *feel* anymore."

One day, after a quiet trip to the mountains, something shifted. She downsized, moved closer to nature, and began choosing meaning over momentum. "I thought I'd feel like I was missing out," she confessed. "But I've never felt richer."

Why We Keep Chasing

The culture we live in thrives on dissatisfaction. It tells us: *You're not enough yet. But buy this, follow this, become this... and maybe you will be.*

This is the myth of more.
It sells **identity** through products, and **self-worth** through external validation.

But our deepest needs belonging, purpose, love cannot be bought.
They can only be lived.

From Seeking to Savoring

So how do we break free from this endless chase?

By learning to **savor** what is, rather than always seeking what could be.

Try this:

- Notice the taste of your food without multitasking.
- Walk slowly. Breathe deeply. Let life move through you.
- Practice gratitude for what already is.
- Ask not "What's next?" but "What's now?"

Example:
A software engineer named Tanya told me she began a 30-day challenge: no online shopping, no social media comparisons, and no new goals. "By

day ten, I started noticing sunlight on my floor. By day twenty, I realized I already had everything I truly needed."

Gentle Reflections

Ask yourself:

- What am I chasing and why?
- Who told me that "more" equals "better"?
- What do I already have that I've been overlooking?

Closing Thought

The myth of more is powerful but it is still a myth.

The truth is simpler, quieter, and far more profound:

You are not behind.
You are not lacking.
You do not need to become someone else to be worthy.

You are already standing in the middle of a life full of beauty, if only you slow down enough to see it.

So, stop running.
Step off the treadmill.

And in that stillness, you may find that what you were chasing was within you all along.

Chapter 7: *Attention Is the New Currency: Reclaiming Focus in the Age of Distraction*

"The greatest of human powers is the power to direct and sustain attention."
— **William James**

There was a time when gold was currency.
Then, it became data.
Now, it is **attention**.

In today's world, the most valuable thing you own is your **focus**
what you choose to see, listen to, and engage with.
Because where your attention goes, **your life flows**.

Yet, in an age of pings, scrolls, and infinite tabs, our attention is constantly being hijacked not by force, but by design.

We are not just distracted.
We are being **trained** to be distracted.

The Economy of Attention

Every app on your phone, every platform you use, every "free" service
is not actually free. **You are the product.**

Your attention is bought and sold in real time.

- Infinite scrolls are engineered to keep you from stopping.
- Notifications are designed to hit your dopamine receptors.
- Algorithms are trained to know your cravings better than you do.

This isn't random. It's **intentional architecture** of your inner world.

Real-life example:
A 2023 study showed that the average adult checks their phone over 90 times a day. That's once every 10 minutes while awake. And yet, most of us can't remember what we saw only how empty we felt afterward.

The Cost of Scattered Minds

What does this endless fragmentation do to us?

- **We lose presence.** Even when we're with loved ones, our minds drift elsewhere.
- **We lose depth.** We skim articles, half-watch shows, and forget halfway through a sentence.
- **We lose agency.** We react more than we respond. We consume more than we create.
- **We lose meaning.** A distracted mind cannot anchor to a deeper purpose.

A distracted life isn't just inefficient it's **shallow**. It becomes harder to love, to work, to pray, to reflect. We become strangers to ourselves.

Ancient Minds, Modern Wounds

Long before smartphones, sages across cultures understood the power of attention.

- In Vedanta, the term *ekagrata* refers to one-pointed concentration considered essential for spiritual growth.
- The Buddha called mindfulness "the path to the deathless."

- In Christian mysticism, attention was a form of devotion *contemplatio*.
- The Stoics spoke of guarding one's inner citadel from the chaos of the outer world.

They knew: **what you focus on, you become**.

Reclaiming Your Inner Light

You don't need to escape the world to reclaim your focus.
You simply need to reclaim **ownership** of your attention.

Here's how:

1. Begin with Mornings

The first 30 minutes of your day shape the quality of your mind.

- Resist the urge to check your phone immediately.
- Instead, sit in stillness. Breathe. Journal. Stretch.
- Let your mind wake up *inside*, not online.

Example:
Neel, a teacher, began starting his mornings with silence and chai on his balcony no screen, just sky. "My anxiety dropped within a week," he shared. "It's like I gave myself back to myself."

2. Single-Task Like a Monk

Multitasking is a myth. Neuroscience has confirmed that what we call multitasking is actually rapid, inefficient switching between tasks.

Try monotasking:

- When you eat, just eat.
- When you talk, just talk.
- When you work, protect that space like sacred ground.

One hour of focused presence is worth five hours of fragmented attention.

3. Create Attention Sanctuaries

Design your environment to support your mind.

- Have tech-free zones: dining tables, bedrooms, nature walks.

- Schedule "do-not-disturb" blocks for deep work or creative flow.
- Turn off unnecessary notifications remember; you are not a fireman on call.

4. Return to the Breath

The breath is the most ancient anchor for attention.

Whenever your mind feels scattered, return to this simple act:

Inhale: I am here.
Exhale: I am now.

Do this for one minute. You have just reclaimed your life.

Gentle Reflections

Ask yourself:

- Who or what is renting space in my mind today?
- What does my attention say about what I value?

- What would it feel like to give my full presence to one thing, right now?

Closing Thought

In a distracted age, attention is not just a tool it is **a form of resistance**.
A way of saying: *I choose what matters. I decide where I live.*
Because attention, at its core, is love.

To give your attention fully to your child, your breath, your work, your prayer is to return to the most human part of yourself.

So, protect your attention.
Not just to be productive.
But to be **present**.
To be **whole**.
To be **alive**.

Chapter 8: *The Sacred Pause: Rediscovering the Power of Doing Nothing*

"It is only when there is no goal and no rush that the human senses are fully open to receive the world."
— Alan Watts

A World Addicted to Motion

We live in a world that worships movement.
We glorify busyness like a badge of honor.
We're told: *If you're not doing something, you're falling behind.*

So, we fill our calendars, our thoughts, and our screens
Afraid of the quiet, terrified of stillness,
as though pausing might cause us to disappear.

But what if the greatest act of rebellion in this overcharged age is not to do more
but to **do nothing**?

To pause.
To breathe.
To exist.

The Forgotten Art of the Pause

In music, it is the **silence between notes** that gives rhythm its shape.
In conversation, it is the **pause** that allows meaning to deepen.
In nature, **winter** is a sacred pause a time when trees look dead, but roots grow deeper.

Yet we, in our modern haste, fear stillness. We equate it with laziness, with being left behind.
We forget that even the heart beats with a pause between beats.
Without the pause there is no life.

The Exhaustion of Constant Doing

Let's be honest: we are tired.

Not just physically, but **existentially**.
We are tired of performing, chasing, proving, comparing.

We open a news feed not to be informed, but to avoid being alone with our thoughts.
We work late, not because we love our work, but

because we're terrified of unstructured time. We fill every empty moment with content scrolling, streaming, swiping never truly resting.

Real-life example:
Priya, a 29-year-old consultant, shared: "Even on weekends, I feel this guilt if I'm not being productive. Rest feels irresponsible. But the truth is I'm just surviving, not living."

The Wisdom of Ancient Cultures

Across centuries, stillness was seen not as indulgence, but as sacred necessity.

- **In Taoism**, *wu wei* refers to "non-doing" or effortless action allowing life to unfold rather than forcing it.
- **In Christianity**, the Sabbath is a holy pause rest not as escape, but as worship.
- **In Hinduism**, the Upanishads speak of *shanti*, not merely as peace, but as the quiet underlying all of reality.
- **Zen Buddhism** teaches *zazen* sitting in stillness not to achieve something, but to remember what you already are.

These traditions whisper the same truth:
Stillness is not the enemy of growth.
It is the **womb** from which growth arises.

The Gift of Doing Nothing

When we allow ourselves to **pause without agenda**, something profound begins to happen:

- Our breath slows.
- Our mind settles.
- Our heart begins to whisper truths we've ignored.
- Our senses open to the miracle of the present.

Doing nothing is not emptiness. It is **presence without pressure**.
It is **being**, without the burden of becoming.

"Sometimes I sits and thinks, and sometimes I just sits."
— Satchel Paige

Stillness in Practice: A Quiet Morning

Imagine this:

You wake up and **don't** reach for your phone.
You sit by the window, tea in hand, watching the morning light shift across the floor.
There is no podcast playing. No list being made.
Just breath, warmth, light.
You are not *preparing* for the day.
You are *inhabiting* it.

In that moment, you are free not because you've accomplished anything, but because you've returned to yourself.

Practical Ways to Invite the Sacred Pause

You don't need a retreat or a monastery.
You need small, consistent spaces in your day to **not do**.

1. The Five-Minute Sit

Once a day, sit in silence no phone, no agenda.
Just breathe and observe.
Let it be awkward. Let it be beautiful.

2. The Slow Walk

Take a walk without destination. No headphones. Just footsteps, wind, and your senses.

3. The Digital Fast

Once a week, go tech-free for 2–3 hours. Let your mind detox from constant input.

4. The Sky Gaze

Lie on your back and watch the sky. Let your thoughts float like clouds.
You are doing nothing and everything.

Gentle Reflections

Ask yourself:

- When was the last time I did nothing without guilt?
- What would happen if I stopped trying to fill every gap?

- What might I hear if I stopped drowning out the silence?

Closing Thought

In a world spinning ever faster, the invitation to pause is radical.

To be still is not to escape life but to re-enter it with awakened senses.
To do nothing is not to waste time but to **touch eternity within time**.
To rest is not to fall behind but to come home.

So rest.
Pause.
Be still.

Let the world spin, while you remember who you are.

Because sometimes, the most meaningful thing you can do is to do nothing at all.

Chapter 9: *The Loneliness Epidemic: Why We're More Connected but Feel More Alone*

"The eternal quest of the human being is to shatter his loneliness."
— Norman Cousins

The Paradox of Our Time

We are the most **connected generation** in human history.

At the tap of a screen, we can talk to someone across the planet, attend virtual events, or broadcast our thoughts to thousands.

And yet beneath this glittering web of notifications and messages
we are lonelier than ever.

This is not a poetic exaggeration.
It is a **silent epidemic**.

A Crisis Hidden in Plain Sight

In a 2023 global survey, over 50% of young adults reported feeling lonely “frequently” or “always.”
Not just alone, but unseen.
Not just disconnected, but **unmoored**.

Psychologists now call loneliness the **new smoking** linked to higher risks of depression, anxiety, dementia, heart disease, and premature death.

But the wound is not just medical.
It is **existential**.

We are suffering not only from the absence of people
but from the absence of *meaningful connection*.

The Illusion of Connection

Social media promised to bring us together. And in some ways, it has.

- Families separated by oceans now share real-time moments.
- Voices once unheard now have platforms.

- Movements can spark across borders in hours.

But there is a shadow.

- **Scrolling** replaces conversation.
- **Likes** replace eye contact.
- **Stories** replace storytelling.
- **Followers** replace friends.

Real-life example:
Raj, a 35-year-old software engineer, shared:
"I have over a thousand LinkedIn contacts, five WhatsApp groups, and Instagram DMs full of memes. But I don't have anyone I can call at 2 a.m. if I'm really in pain."

That sentence echoes a silent ache across the modern soul.

The Deep Psychology of Loneliness

Humans are wired for connection.
From infancy, we seek attunement someone who mirrors our emotions, who says, *"I see you. I hear you. You matter."*

When we are deprived of this, something within us begins to dissolve:

- Our sense of **belonging** fades.
- Our sense of **worth** weakens.
- Our ability to **trust and be vulnerable** erodes.

Loneliness is not just emptiness.
It is the **pain of unshared being**.

Belonging: The Antidote to Loneliness

What we seek is not more contacts, but **more connection**.
Not more followers, but **more fellowship**.

Belonging does not come from fitting in it comes from **being seen as you are**.

Pathways Back to Real Connection

How do we begin to heal from this loneliness in the age of hyper-connectivity?

1. Practice Deep Listening

When someone speaks, listen not to respond but to **receive**.
Put away the phone. Let silence exist between words.

Offer your full presence. It is a rare and sacred gift.

Presence is the purest form of love.

2. Reclaim Small Communions

Not every connection must be deep but every moment of kindness counts.

- Greet your neighbors.
- Share meals.
- Compliment a stranger.
- Be curious about others, not just their opinions.

Real-life example:
Sara, a college student struggling with loneliness, began volunteering at a community kitchen. "The simple act of serving food and hearing stories pulled me out of my shell," she said. "I remembered that I was part of something larger than my loneliness."

3. Spend Time in Shared Stillness

Loneliness is not always healed by talking it can be healed by **being** with others.

- Sit in nature with a friend.

- Walk without agenda.
- Meditate in silence.
- Be alone *together*.

This is not socializing.
It is **soul presence**.

4. Reach Out First

Sometimes, we wait for others to invite us, to notice us, to care.
But what if we made the first move?

- Text that old friend.
- Write a letter to someone who made a difference.
- Call just to say: *"I'm thinking of you."*

Loneliness shrinks in the light of initiative.

Gentle Reflections

Ask yourself:

- What does meaningful connection look like for me?
- When do I feel most seen and safe?

- Who in my life might be silently lonely and how might I reach them?

Closing Thought

Loneliness is not a weakness. It is a **signal** a sacred longing for reconnection.

It tells us: *I want to belong.*
I want to matter.
I want to be known, not just noticed.

And here's the grace: you're not alone in that.

Everyone is carrying some version of this ache.
Everyone is hoping someone else will say hello first.

So let us begin again
With small kindnesses, with shared stillness, with the courage to be real.

Because in the end, connection is not found through more noise
but through quiet presence.
Not through more updates
but through deeper conversations.
Not through more "likes"
but through *more love.*

Chapter 10: *The Age of Overwhelm: Navigating Chaos Without Losing Yourself*

"You are not required to set yourself on fire to keep others warm."
— Anonymous

The Tidal Wave Within

There's a word that hangs in the background of nearly every conversation today:
Overwhelm.

It's the slow suffocation of too much
Too many choices.
Too many tabs open in our minds.
Too many voices demanding our attention.
Too many expectations, notifications, ambitions, comparisons.

We wake up exhausted, and go to sleep restless.
We're productive, yet feel perpetually behind.
We're connected, yet feel frayed.
We're doing everything, but becoming no one.

A Culture of Constant Crisis

This is not just personal it's cultural.
We are raised in a system that rewards burnout and glorifies hustle.

- **Emails don't sleep.**
- **Deadlines breathe down our necks.**
- **News cycles spin endlessly.**
- **Social media bombards us with lives we think we should be living.**

And underneath it all, we ask ourselves:

How am I supposed to keep up?

But perhaps the better question is:

Why must I keep up with a world that doesn't know how to slow down?

The Consequences of Living Overwhelmed

Chronic overwhelm does more than stress us out.
It **shrinks our soul**.

- We lose clarity.
- We forget our values.
- We snap at people we love.
- We move from task to task, but forget *why* we began.

Overwhelm is not just too much to do.
It's **too little space to be**.

The Psychology Behind Overwhelm

Neuroscience tells us the brain is designed to process a limited amount of information at a time. When overloaded, it shifts into survival mode:

- Fight
- Flight
- Freeze
- Fawn

We become reactive rather than responsive.
We multitask poorly.
We numb out.
We disconnect.

And worst of all: we stop hearing the voice of our own intuition.

Real-Life Glimpse

Arjun, a 37-year-old marketing professional, said: "There are days I open my laptop and I can't even breathe. I'm juggling five meetings, parenting, emails, and trying to grow on LinkedIn. I feel like I'm everywhere except in myself."

His story is not rare.
It is *representative*.

The Antidote to Overwhelm: Inner Spaciousness

We often think the solution to overwhelm is better time management.
But what we really need is **inner spaciousness**.

A sense of groundedness.
A return to breath.
A reconnection to what is *essential*.

"Beware the barrenness of a busy life."
— Socrates

The cure is not in doing more with less time.
It is doing **less**, more mindfully with presence, not pressure.

Ways to Navigate Chaos with Clarity

1. Create Sacred Spaces of No-Input

Carve out times in your day when you allow no new information in.

- No phone.
- No notifications.
- No noise.

Sit in the quiet and let your nervous system reset. This is not a luxury. It's maintenance for your mind.

2. Ask the Golden Question: "Is This Essential?"

Before saying yes, before reacting, before rushing ask:

"Is this essential, or am I just afraid of being irrelevant?"

Let that question cut through the fog.

3. Single-Task with Sacred Attention

Multitasking is a myth.
Choose one task. Give it your whole presence.

- When eating, just eat.
- When walking, just walk.
- When talking, just listen.

You will regain your rhythm and your soul.

4. Anchor to Your Breath

Your breath is always with you.
And it's always in the present.

When you feel overwhelmed, pause.
Inhale deeply. Exhale slowly.
Let your breath become your compass back to stillness.

5. Let Go of the Unnecessary

Overwhelm is often not from *what* we carry, but *how much.*

- Unfollow accounts that exhaust you.
- Say no with love and without guilt.

- Cancel obligations that no longer align with your heart.

Free space. Free mind. Free self.

Gentle Reflections

Ask yourself:

- Where in my life am I overcommitted but undernourished?
- What would I do if I believed that rest was productive?
- Who am I trying to impress and is it worth my peace?

Closing Thought

You are not a machine.
You are not a project.
You are not a brand.

You are a soul
sensitive, radiant, rhythmic, alive.

The world will always shout, “Do more. Be more. Prove more.”
But in the quiet, your heart whispers:

Come back. Slow down. You are already enough.

Overwhelm is not your destiny.
Stillness is your birthright.

In the storm of modern life, your power lies not in pushing harder
but in **pausing wisely**.

Let that pause become your revolution.

Chapter 11: *The Lost Art of Presence: How to Truly Be Where You Are*

"Wherever you are, be there totally."
— Eckhart Tolle

The Great Disappearance

We live in a time of astonishing access: to people, places, ideas, entertainment.

But in all this gain, something precious has quietly vanished
Our presence.

We're everywhere… but not here.
We're connected… but not available.
We're busy… but not alive in the moment.

We scroll while eating, plan while talking, worry while walking.
The now becomes background noise.
The people in front of us become secondary to the screens in our hands.
Our thoughts scatter like birds startled by the wind.

And in that distraction, we lose something vital: **Ourselves.**

What Is Presence, Really?

Presence is **not** just physical nearness.
It is **mental stillness**, **emotional attunement**, and **soulful attention**.

To be present is:

- To listen with your whole being.
- To breathe in the moment without resisting or escaping.
- To experience life **directly**, not filtered through commentary, comparison, or agenda.

Presence is not a performance.
It is a **return** to what is real, right now.

Real-Life Story: The Dinner Table Awakening

Maya, a working mother of two, shared a simple but powerful story:
"One evening, I was sitting at dinner with my kids. I was answering emails on my phone, half-hearing their stories. My daughter, only seven, looked at

me and said:
'Mommy, you're not really here.'

That sentence shattered me. From that day on, I started leaving my phone in another room during meals. Slowly, I learned how to *be there* again. And I saw how starved we all were for each other's full attention."

The Cost of Absence

When we are not present, we suffer in subtle ways:

- **Conversations become noise.**
- **Beauty passes us by.**
- **We forget the joy of simple moments.**
- **Our minds stay tethered to past regrets and future anxieties.**

We miss the life that's happening while we chase a version of life, we think we should be living.

Presence is not just about peace.
It's about **participation in our own lives**.

Why Presence Feels So Elusive

Presence seems simple, yet it often feels impossible. Why?

1. **Overstimulated Minds**
   Our brains are bombarded daily by content, decisions, distractions. We are trained to jump from one thing to the next and we mistake this hyperactivity for productivity.

2. **Unprocessed Emotions**
   Being present brings us face to face with ourselves. Many avoid presence because it brings up feelings, we haven't resolved sadness, boredom, fear, grief.

3. **Addiction to Escape**
   Entertainment, news, scrolling, constant talking all are ways we numb ourselves from the stillness that presence demands.

4. **Fear of Missing Out (FOMO)**
   We're terrified that by committing to this moment, we're missing something better elsewhere. So, we stay half-here, half-there and fully nowhere.

Cultivating Presence: The Everyday Practice of Returning

Presence is not achieved.
It is **returned to**, again and again, like a gentle homecoming.

Here's how we begin:

1. Anchor to the Breath

Your breath is the most honest part of you.
It is always in the present moment.

- Notice the inhale.
- Feel the exhale.
- Let it ground you in *now*.

Even 30 seconds of breath-awareness can reset your nervous system and bring your awareness home.

2. Slow One Thing Down Daily

Pick one ordinary act and do it slowly and mindfully.

- Drink your tea without a phone.

- Walk without earbuds.
- Wash dishes while feeling the water.

Let the *ordinary* become *sacred*.

3. Offer Full Attention

When someone speaks to you, practice full presence.

- Maintain soft eye contact.
- Listen without preparing your reply.
- Hold silence without rushing to fill it.

You'll find people soften in your presence because being fully heard is healing.

4. Take Mini Digital Sabbaths

Even a 10-minute break from screens each day can restore inner quiet.

- Step outside.
- Sit under a tree.
- Breathe.

- Observe the world unfolding without needing to capture or share it.

Reclaim the joy of unrecorded life.

5. Name This Moment

Try this simple practice:
Pause. Breathe. Ask yourself:

"What is here, right now?"

Feel your body.
Notice your thoughts.
Observe the surroundings.
And simply say:
"This is what now feels like."

Gentle Reflections

- When was the last time I was truly present with myself, with someone, with life?

- What prevents me from being here now?

- Can I practice the art of deep attention, without needing to fix or judge?

Closing Thought

Presence is not something to strive for.
It is something to **surrender into**.

It is not about doing more
but about **being more fully in what you're already doing**.

In a world screaming for your attention, presence is your silent rebellion.
In an age of speed, presence is your sanctuary.
And in the storm of endless distractions, presence is the still point that reminds you:

You are already home.
You don't need to chase the moment. You are the moment.

Return to it.
And in doing so, you return to yourself.

Chapter 12: *The Myth of More: Why Fulfillment Isn't Found in Excess*

"It is not the man who has too little, but the man who craves more, that is poor."
— Seneca

The Age of Accumulation

We are constantly told to want more.

- More money.
- More success.
- More followers.
- More productivity.
- More excitement.
- More of *everything*.

We are taught to measure our lives by quantity of achievements, of possessions, of attention. The world whispers:

You'll be happy when you have more.

So, we chase relentlessly, breathlessly.
We climb ladders we never questioned.
We collect things we don't need to impress people we don't know.
We run faster, only to feel emptier.

And somewhere along the way, we forget to ask the most important question:

More of what? And at what cost?

The Psychology of "More"

At the heart of this myth is a psychological trap known as the **hedonic treadmill** a well-researched concept in behavioural psychology. It describes how we adapt to new pleasures quickly, making them feel ordinary, and then crave the *next* thing to feel good again.

It's why:

- A new car thrills us for a week, then feels normal.
- A raise excites us briefly, but doesn't last.
- The perfect vacation fades into memory, replaced by the need for another escape.

We are biologically wired to pursue growth and novelty but when left unchecked, this drive becomes **greed, restlessness, and chronic dissatisfaction**.

Real-Life Snapshot: The Empty Victory

Karan, a tech entrepreneur, built a successful app that went viral. He became wealthy overnight. But within a year, he said:

"I thought having more would silence the anxiety inside me. But it only got louder. The fame faded, the money didn't fulfil me, and I realised … I had climbed the wrong mountain."

Karan's story is not rare. It echoes across boardrooms, social feeds, and quiet minds everywhere.

The Inversion: Less is Often More

The ancient philosophies from Stoicism to Vedanta, from Buddhism to minimalism speak the same truth:

Freedom lies not in having more, but in needing less.

Real fulfillment doesn't come from **expanding our desires**, but from **refining them**.

What if:

- Simplicity was a form of wealth?
- Contentment was a radical act?
- Having *enough* was actually the new success?

Cultivating a Life Beyond "More"

Let us explore how to step off the treadmill and root ourselves in **what truly matters**.

1. Redefine Success

Instead of asking, *"What more can I get?"*, ask:

"What do I truly value?"
"What do I want to be remembered for?"

Success is not accumulation.
It is **alignment** living in harmony with your soul's purpose.

2. Practice Grateful Minimalism

Gratitude turns what we have into enough. Minimalism doesn't mean owning nothing. It means owning only what adds value to your life.

Start small:

- Declutter your space.
- Unsubscribe from digital noise.
- Let go of relationships that drain your energy.
- Keep only what brings peace, depth, and usefulness.

3. Savor, Don't Accumulate

Instead of hoarding experiences, **savor them**.

- Slow down your meals.
- Sit longer with sunsets.
- Read one book deeply instead of ten quickly.
- Give people your full presence.

Fulfillment grows in depth, not volume.

4. Cut the Invisible Costs of "More"

Every "more" we chase has a hidden price:

- More work → less time for family.
- More screens → less sleep.

- More speed → less peace.
- More consumption → less awareness.

Ask often: *What am I trading for this?*
If the cost is your peace, the price is too high.

5. Embrace the Power of Enough

“Enough” is a sacred word.

It means:

I have what I need.
I am not lacking.
I choose to rest in sufficiency.

Living with “enough” isn’t giving up ambition it’s giving up **attachment**.

Gentle Reflections

- In which areas of life am I chasing “more” without clarity or joy?
- What would it look like to live from a place of sufficiency rather than scarcity?
- Can I practice choosing depth over width, quality over quantity?

Closing Thought

The modern world may celebrate excess but your soul doesn't.

Your soul is simple, still, and wise.
It craves meaning, not accumulation.
It yearns for peace, not applause.

When we stop sprinting toward "more," we begin to walk toward ourselves.
We return to what is real.
We begin to live **awake**.

So pause. Breathe.
And let go of what you don't need.

Because sometimes, the most beautiful life isn't one filled with *everything*
but one filled with just **enough** of what truly matters.

Chapter 13: *A Quiet Revolution: Choosing Meaning in the Noise*

One Storm, Many Journeys

You've made it to the final pages of this book not by accident, but because something in you longed to remember a forgotten truth.

That your life is not measured by the number of tasks completed, tabs opened, or applause received.
But by how **present** you were.
How **awake** you felt.
How **kindly** you lived.
And how often you touched the sacred within the ordinary.

In the great storm of the modern world of information overload, relentless productivity, digital intoxication, and existential fatigue you've sought not escape, but **essence**.

And that is a quiet revolution in itself.

The Call Beneath the Noise

This age is loud. It is restless, hurried, distracted. But beneath the noise, life is still whispering.

It is whispering in the early morning stillness.
In the laughter of your child.
In the breeze through the window.
In the ache of your heart asking, "Is there more?"

And here's the truth:

There is more. But not more to achieve or acquire more to awaken.

More meaning.
More clarity.
More connection.
More peace.

But they are not found "out there."
They are discovered by slowing down, looking in, and *living from the center outward.*

The Compass Within

This journey was never about finding some grand secret.

It was about **remembering** what the world made us forget:

- That silence heals.
- That presence transforms.
- That meaning isn't given it is **made** through intention, attention, and alignment.
- That our greatest technology is not in our hands, but in our hearts.
- That we are not here to be *busy*, but to be **awake**.

You don't need to renounce the world.
You simply need to return to yourself in it.

Real-Life Glimpse: A Quiet Shift

Aarav, a corporate strategist, didn't leave his job to find peace.
He simply changed *how* he showed up.

He started walking without his phone.
He meditated 10 minutes before work.
He listened deeply in meetings instead of multitasking.
He learned to say "no" to protect his "yes."

In six months, his anxiety dropped. His relationships deepened. And his joy the quiet, steady kind returned.

The world didn't change. But *he* did.
And that was enough.

What the Storm Teaches

Storms don't just bring destruction.
They reveal what cannot be shaken.

This book has been a guide not to shelter you from the chaos, but to help you stand **still** within it.

In that stillness, you'll find:

- Your own rhythm.
- Your own wisdom.
- And the courage to live in a way that is gentle, grounded, and real.

Because meaning is not a destination. It is a *daily devotion.*

Final Reflections for the Soul

- What would it look like to live more *deliberately* and less reactively?
- What do I already have that I keep overlooking?
- How can I bring more soul into my schedule, and more presence into my days?

Parting Words: Live Lightly, Live Deeply

May you walk through the noise without becoming it.
May you create space for silence not as an escape, but as a source.
May you pause often, breathe deeply, and remember:

You are not behind.
You are not late.
You are exactly where the story needs you to awaken.

You don't need to do more to be enough.
You don't need to prove your worth by exhaustion.
You don't need to run.

You are allowed
to rest,
to wonder,
to choose depth over speed,
and to live a life that *feels like yours*.

Let this book not end here, but begin anew within you.
In how you wake up.
In how you pay attention.
In how you love.
In how you live.

Because the real revolution in a distracted world…
Is a quiet, meaningful, *fully conscious life*.

Stillness is not a pause.
It is your power.

Return to it.

And from there,
Live.

Epilogue: A Whisper to the Soul

"And you? When will you begin that long journey into yourself?"
— Rumi

No storm lasts forever.
But while it rages, it teaches.

It strips away the noise, the pretending, the striving
Until all that remains is you.
Still.
Silent.
Whole.

This book was never meant to be a map,
but a **mirror**
Reflecting back the truth you always carried.

That meaning is not something you must chase.
It is something you uncover
in stillness,
in wonder,
in presence,
in love.

So as the last page turns,
carry this with you:

You are allowed to unplug,
to breathe,
to choose a slower rhythm in a faster world.
To walk the unbeaten path.
To live with eyes open and heart grounded.

Let your life not be a blur of busy,
but a poem of presence.

Not a performance,
but a practice.

Not just survival,
but soul.

And if ever you forget
return to the stillness.

It will always be there.

Waiting.

www.ingramcontent.com/pod-product-compliance
Ingram Content Group UK Ltd.
Pitfield, Milton Keynes, MK11 3LW, UK
UKHW041348190726
13845UKWH00026B/476

9 789334 274516